YOUR DOMESTIC WORKER AND THE LAW

YOUR DOMESTIC WORKER AND THE LAW

MATTHEW GROSSETT

SOUTHERN
BOOK PUBLISHERS

ISBN 1 86812 541 6

First edition, first impression 1994

Published by
Southern Book Publishers (Pty) Ltd
PO Box 3103, Halfway House, 1685

Cover design by Abdul Amien
Typography by Wim Reinders & Associates, Cape Town
Set in 10/12 Palatino by 4-Ways DTP Services, Cape Town
Printed and bound by Sigma Press, Pretoria

Contents

Preface

Since the Basic Conditions of Employment Act was extended to cover domestic workers, the nature of the relationship between employer and domestic worker has changed drastically. The object of this text is to provide an overview of the latest developments in the domestic's employment arena. In writing this book, I have tried as far as possible to present the information in an uncomplicated style, while integrating the common law of employment with the Basic Conditions of Employment as applicable to domestic workers.

This text is not intended as a reference for lawyers, but is intended to be a concise and practical reference book for students, employers and domestics alike.

The purpose of this book is not to reproduce in full the texts of industrial legislation and regulations but to provide summaries highlighting important aspects. In addition, the text contains practical guidelines for the procedures to be followed by the parties to the employment contract in preventing or dealing with problems which may arise out of the association.

Please note that because most domestic workers are female and they usually report to the woman of the household, both employers and employees are referred to as "she" in this book.

I trust that you will find this text a practical and useful reference, and that it will contribute to harmonious working relationships in many homes.

Brief though it is, I needed a lot of help and support in writing this book. I benefited greatly from the insights of many people – too many to mention – and from their patience while I bounced ideas off them and their comments on the early manuscripts.

To Felicity Thomas, who by her continual encouragement gave me the courage and belief to tackle this project, thank you.

Thanks also to Raylene, who assisted me greatly in the typing of the manuscript.

Thank you to my wife Kim, for your patience, understanding and unfailing support and interest. Without you this task would have been much more daunting.

Matthew Grossett Johannesburg

Help-line

Should the reader have questions not answered in this text, contact me by phone, fax or post. You'll receive an answer within 48 hours of your request. This service is available free of charge.

Contact address:
Mr Matthew Grossett
Department of Business Economics
Private Bag 3
Wits
2050

Contact telephone number:
(011) 716-5206

Contact fax number:
(011) 339-7385

1. Introduction

For the first time in the history of South Africa, domestic workers are provided with some protection under labour law. Until January 1994, the only protection offered to domestics was that provided by the common law, more specifically, the contract of employment. As from 1 January 1994, basic working rights, contained in the Basic Conditions of Employment Act (No 3 of 1983, as amended), have been granted to domestic workers.

The application of the Act changes totally the relationship between employer and domestic worker, placing that relationship on a legal basis for the first time. The Act covers every aspect of domestic workers' employment, placing them on a contractual basis similar to that of workers in the formal sector.

The purpose of this book is to focus on the essential things you need to know about the law as it affects you and your domestic worker. It provides an easy to understand interpretation of the law as it applies to domestics. An important principle of this text is to provide easy to follow, practical explanations of the implications of the law for the employer of a domestic worker. This will make the employer and the domestic aware of what their rights and obligations in the employment relationship are, in addition to providing information on the various courses of action available to the parties should any of these rights be breached.

Chapter 2 provides all the definitions necessary to make sense of the Act. Chapters 3 and 4 are a simplified version of the law itself as it applies to the parties to the relationship. Included in these chapters is an explanation of the duties and obligations of the employer and domestic worker. Chapter 5 deals with the contract of employment, a document that is central to the employment relationship. Chapter 6 deals with the procedures that need to be followed when either disciplining or dismissing a domestic worker. Chapter 7 explains the various methods whereby either the employer or the domestic may terminate the working relationship. Chapter 8 provides an explanation of the various options open to either the employer or her domestic, should the terms and conditions of the contract not be adhered to. Chapter 9 is a summary of the more important elements of the law and how it affects domestic workers and their employers. It is intended to serve as a quick reference to problems or questions that may arise during the course of the employment relationship. Chapter 10 deals with the disciplinary procedure.

2. Definitions

In terms of the Act, the following people are considered to fall under the broad definition of "domestic workers" and are accordingly covered by the law.

Domestic servants. Included here is any person who, inter alia, is involved in:
- □ cleaning and washing the contents of a private household
- □ washing and ironing bed linen, towels, clothing and so on in a private household
- □ preparing and cooking meals for the household and guests
- □ washing up after meals.

Gardeners. Included here is any person who, inter alia:
- □ maintains the garden of a private household, including watering, mowing, raking, digging flower beds, etc.
- □ keeps the swimming pool clean

Household chauffeurs. Included here is any person who, inter alia:
- □ drives members of a private household to and from specific places
- □ delivers and collects groceries or other goods
- □ performs duties such as collecting and delivering post, etc.

Childminders. Included here is any person who, inter alia:
- □ supervises the children of a private household
- □ babysits the children of a private household
- □ prepares children's meals.

Those who care for the sick, aged or frail. Included in this category is any person who is in any way involved in looking after an elderly or sick person in a private household.

It is important to note that although a person may be fulfilling one or more of the above functions, to be considered a domestic worker, the following two requirements must be satisfied:
- □ The person must be employed in a *private* household.

- □ This household should be mainly a dwelling place, as opposed to a business.

There are several different categories of domestics or employees:

- □ Full-time workers residing on the property.
- □ Full-time workers who do not reside on the property (non-residents).
- □ Regular day workers or, as they are more often known, part-time workers. To qualify as a part-time worker, the worker may not be employed for more than three days in any one week for a period of not less than four consecutive weeks.
- □ Casual workers. To qualify as a casual worker, the worker may only work for three days a week or less, for a period of less than one month. Should this practice exceed one month (working for three days a week or less) then the worker would be defined as a regular day worker or part-time worker.

What do you do if you need casual labour for a longer period (for example, for the time during which your regular domestic is away on leave)? Employ a person temporarily for a fixed period. Ensure that there is a clear understanding that the job is temporary, starting on a specific date and ending on a specific date. You should record these details in writing, along with the amount you intend to pay.

It is important to be aware of the different categories of domestics, as the law often lays down different conditions for persons in the different categories. Where these differences occur, they will be brought to the reader's attention.

3. *Legal obligations of the employer*

Until 1 January 1994, the relationship between an employer and her domestic worker was governed solely by the common law. Prior to this date, this class of worker had no statutory protection. As of 1 January 1994, the Basic Conditions of Employment Act (BCEA) was extended to include domestic workers. The relationship between an employer and her domestic worker is governed by both the BCEA and the common law. As a general rule, the common law is superseded by the BCEA, *unless* the agreement between the parties is more beneficial to the employee/domestic. For example, the BCEA stipulates that a domestic worker has the right to 14 days' paid leave per annum. Any agreement between you and your domestic (even a written contract) which stipulates a lesser period (say 10 days) would not be valid and binding, and would be superseded by the BCEA, mandating 14 days. Assume however that you enter into an agreement with your domestic for her to have 21 days' paid leave annually. Because this agreement is more beneficial to the employee than the provisions of the BCEA (21 days as opposed to 14 days), the employer would be contractually bound by the contents of such agreement.

Before embarking on an explanation of the duties and obligations of the employer and her domestic to each other, it is important to be aware of the origins of these duties and obligations. There are two prime sources which determine the reciprocal rights and obligations of employer and employee/domestic worker:

- the common law
- the Basic Conditions of Employment Act.

The duties and obligations of the parties may be either explicitly contained in a contract of employment or they may form an implicit part of the contract. The implications of this are that the absence of certain stipulations from the formal contract of employment between an employer and her domestic worker does not mean that the parties are not bound by such stipulations. For example, the absence of a clause stipulating that the employer is required to provide safe working conditions does not absolve her of her duty to do so. The reason is that, although not expressly contained in the contract of employment, the employer has an implicit duty to provide safe working conditions for her domestic worker/s.

In terms of the law, every employer has a number of duties towards her employee/domestic. These duties are detailed either explicitly or implicitly in both the common law and the BCEA.

Before proceeding to discuss these duties and obligations, it is important to establish first whether you have an employer-employee relationship with your domestic or not. If such a relationship does exist, then you are an *employer* and accordingly fall under the scope of the law. For the relationship between two or more parties to be considered an employer-employee relationship, the overall impression should be one of a "master-servant" relationship between the two parties. The following factors will strongly indicate the existence of a master-servant relationship:

- ☐ The employer supervisers:
  - — what work is to be done by the domestic
  - — the manner in which the domestic does the work
- ☐ The employer determines the working hours of the domestic.
- ☐ The employer provides all or most of the tools and equipment used by the domestic worker to do her job.

Having established that you are an employer (i.e. an employer-employee relationship exists), it now becomes pertinent to investigate what the rights and obligations of the employer are. The duties and obligations of an employer, as contained in the common law and the BCEA, are:

- ☐ to observe prescribed hours of work
- ☐ to observe overtime regulations
- ☐ to observe meal intervals
- ☐ to pay remuneration
- ☐ to provide safe working conditions
- ☐ to provide annual leave
- ☐ to provide sick leave
- ☐ to provide a certificate of service
- ☐ to acknowledge public holidays
- ☐ to employ only certain persons
- ☐ not to victimise employees
- ☐ to observe the prohibition of certain acts relating to the payment of remuneration
- ☐ to keep prescribed records
- ☐ to facilitate inspections.

3.1 Prescribed hours of work

Common law. Under the common law it is up to the parties to regulate the employee's working hours. If their agreement makes no provision for maximum hours of work, then the hours will be regulated by custom. Employers may not exact unreasonable hours of work from employees.

In the absence of any agreement or statute to the contrary, where maximum hours of work are stipulated in the agreement, the employer may require the employee to work overtime when circumstances require.

Labour law. As regards domestic workers, working hours and overtime are however regulated by statute, and accordingly it is not up to the parties to agree on the maximum hours of work, unless of course the agreement between the parties reduces the maximum work time or overtime to less than the amount stipulated in the statutes.

In terms of the Basic Conditions of Employment Act, the normal working week may not be longer than 46 hours. Further, the BCEA stipulates that the maximum number of hours that an employer is permitted to allow a domestic to work per day is nine hours and 15 minutes for domestics working a five-day week and not more than eight hours per day for domestics who work six days per week. A domestic working a six-day week may, in the case of her working for five hours or less on a particular day, work up to eight hours and 30 minutes on any of the other days. The above hours of work can be extended by overtime work, for which a domestic is paid at a higher stipulated rate (see paragraph 3.2).

In determining the time worked by a domestic in one week:

- The time worked on a Sunday shall be disregarded.
- The time taken up by meal intervals shall be disregarded.
- Any overtime worked during that week not exceeding the maximum permissible weekly amount of overtime shall be disregarded.

As regards regular day workers/part-time workers (persons working up to three days a week) and casual workers (persons working not more than three days a week and whose total period of employment with the same employer is not more than a month) the maximum permissible number of work hours per day is nine hours and 15 minutes.

In addition to the above basic guidelines to working hours, there are a number of important prescriptions which should be noted.

3.1.1 Maximum length of the working day

As regulated by the BCEA, the working day of a full-time domestic may not be spread over more than 14 hours for live-in workers, or 12 hours for non-resident workers. The term "spread over" refers to the period of time from the start of the work day until finishing time. Accordingly, if a domestic starts work at 8h00, her work day must end by 20h00 (including all meal intervals, overtime, etc). If the domestic had worked such hours, her day will have been spread over 12 hours, but the actual time worked may have been only nine hours, with a three-hour break in the middle of the day.

As indicated, the BCEA stipulates the maximum permissible hours of work. However, the parties may negotiate and consequently be bound by working hours different from those stipulated in the Act, as long as the end figure agreed upon does not exceed the statutory maximum.

3.1.2 The extension of normal working hours

The normal working hours of a domestic worker may, under certain circumstances, be extended. It is possible to arrange that domestic workers work a 52-hour week for a period of up to 26 days in any one year. This can be done provided that for a similar period during the same year they work a 44-hour week. This arrangement must be agreed to in writing and signed by both parties.

3.2 Overtime

The only instance in which an employer can insist that a domestic work overtime (time over and above the normal hours of work as stipulated by the BCEA) is when both parties have agreed to the working of such overtime.

The BCEA stipulates the maximum amount of overtime which may be worked on any one day and in any one week. The Act stipulates that a domestic may not be required to work more than three hours of overtime on any one day or more than 10 hours in any one week. The Act does however make provision for the 10-hour limitation to be extended to 14 hours in cases where the domestic is employed to look after children, the frail or the sick.

If, however, the parties have agreed to an extended work week (52 hours), the Act limits daily overtime to two hours and the weekly total to six hours.

3.3 Meal intervals

The BCEA stipulates that a domestic may not work for more than five hours continuously without being given a meal break of not less than one hour. By mutual agreement between the two parties, however, this break may be shortened to not less than 30 minutes. Should the parties agree to a shortened meal interval, a domestic working normal time would finish the day the equivalent length of time earlier.

Meal breaks are not considered as work time, and accordingly are unpaid. They do not contribute towards the number of hours worked on a particular day or in a particular week.

A domestic worker employed to look after children, the sick or frail may need to interrupt the meal break to attend to duties. Provided the worker is allowed alternative time for a meal, this is acceptable and no extra payment is required because of the interrupted break.

3.4 Remuneration

Common law. Under the common law, the employer is under an obligation to pay the employee upon the performance of her duties. There are a number of means that can be used to determine the amount of compensation to be received:

- ☐ The two parties may have agreed to the payment of a certain amount of remuneration. The most obvious form that this agreement may take is that of a written contract which expressly contains the amount of remuneration to be paid.
- ☐ Although a final figure of remuneration may not have been agreed, a means to calculate this figure may have been agreed. For example, a part-time worker and her employer may have agreed to a certain hourly rate, thereby facilitating the calculation of the total wage due.
- ☐ Although in the past there may have been no agreement between the employer and the domestic as to the amount of wages to be paid, the employer may for a period of time have been paying the employee a certain wage. In the absence of any agreement to the contrary, where this practice has persisted for some time (usually three months or three payments or more) without the disagreement of either party, then the wage paid will be an implied term of the contract and the domestic will have a right to insist on it.
- ☐ Where no mention is made of the amount of remuneration to be paid and it is not possible to calculate it, the domestic must be

paid a fair amount of remuneration. This amount would be determined by considering what other domestics working in the same vicinity, with similar experience, length of service and job description, are being remunerated.

Labour law. At present, legislation does not stipulate a minimum wage for domestic workers. Therefore the employer of a domestic worker is bound by the common law requirements regarding the amount of remuneration.

3.4.1 Payment in kind

It is important to note that the wage to be paid to a domestic worker may include payment in kind and may include food, accommodation, clothing, electricity and water, travelling costs and schooling of children. Payment in kind is any payment, other than cash, made to the domestic. The BCEA stipulates that in instances where the domestic worker receives part of her remuneration in the form of payment in kind, the monthly value of this form of payment be R100, or an amount agreed upon in writing by the employer and employee, whichever is the greater.

The BCEA, although not stipulating a minimum wage, does make a number of provisions pertaining to the payment of remuneration. The Act regulates:

- □ the manner in which remuneration must be paid
- □ payment for overtime work
- □ payment for work on Sundays
- □ payment for work on public holidays.

3.4.2 The manner in which remuneration must be paid

The BCEA states that any amount due to a domestic shall be paid in *cash*, weekly, fortnightly or monthly or, with the consent of the domestic, by cheque during the hours of work or within 15 minutes of ceasing work on the day agreed upon between the employer and the domestic for such payment (or in the case of a casual worker, at a time agreed upon between the employer and the domestic, which time shall be during the usual work hours of the household). On termination of employment, if this takes place before the pay day agreed upon, such amount shall be accompanied by a statement containing:

- □ the employer's name
- □ the domestic's name and her occupation
- □ the period in respect of which payment is made

- ☐ the number of ordinary hours worked by the domestic
- ☐ the number of overtime hours worked by the domestic
- ☐ the domestic's wage
- ☐ details of any other remuneration arising out of the domestic's employment
- ☐ details of any deductions made
- ☐ the actual amount paid to the domestic.

For a more detailed discussion of the above document, see paragraph 3.14.3.

3.4.3 Payment for overtime work

As you will recall, the BCEA stipulates that a domestic may not be required to work more than 10 hours of overtime in any one week, or more than three hours on any one day. The Act does however make provision for the 10-hour limitation to be extended to 14 hours in cases where the domestic is employed to look after children, the frail or the sick. If however the parties have agreed to an extended work week (52 hours), then the Act limits daily overtime to two hours and the weekly total to six hours.

The BCEA stipulates that any domestic who works overtime must be paid *not less* than one and a third times her normal hourly rate. It is important that this hourly rate be calculated on the basis of the total value of her pay package. The total value of a domestic's pay includes:

- ☐ normal wage/salary, plus
- ☐ the monetary value of any payment in kind, such as food, clothing and accommodation.

It should be noted that where the parties have agreed to an overtime rate higher than the one stipulated by the BCEA (for example double-time) the common law contract (agreement) would supersede the BCEA and the higher amount would be contractually binding on the parties.

The accompanying example illustrates how one would go about calculating the hourly overtime rate.

3.4.4 Payment for work on Sundays

It is important to know the actual number of hours worked on Sundays. The calculation for Sunday pay is done using either one of the following two methods, each of which allows the employer a degree of choice as to the method of compensation.

1. Assume a normal monthly salary of	R 550,00
2. Assume that the domestic is a full-time employee who lives on the property. The BCEA stipulates that the minimum value which may be attached to this payment in kind is to be not less than R100,00 (or any greater amount agreed to by the 2 parties) Monthly wage: cash	R100,00 R550,00
TOTAL VALUE OF MONTHLY PACKAGE	**R650,00**
3. Assume that the domestic works 46 hours per week, or 184 hours per month (assuming four weeks). Accordingly, the normal hourly rate would be R650 divided by 184	R3,53
The overtime rate should be at least one and a third times the normal hourly rate of R3,53	**R4,70**

Method A. If a domestic worker works on a Sunday for four hours or less, she must be paid a normal (full) day's pay.
If, however, a domestic worker works for more than four hours on a Sunday, then she must be paid the greater of either:

- double a normal day's wage, or
- double her normal hourly rate for the number of hours worked on the Sunday.

Method B. Rather than compensate a domestic who worked on a Sunday as described in method A, the BCEA allows one to pay a flat overtime rate (i.e. one and a third times the normal hourly rate) plus give the domestic one full day off on full pay (normal rate) within seven days of having worked the Sunday.

3.4.5 Public holidays and payment for work on public holidays
As prescribed by the BCEA, the following are the only paid public holidays applicable to domestic workers:
New Year's Day

Good Friday
Workers' Day
Ascension Day
Republic Day
Day of the Vow
Christmas Day

Regarding payment for work on public holidays, one needs to differentiate between a public holiday which falls on a normal working day and a public holiday which falls on a day that is not a normal working day for the domestic (e.g. a Sunday, assuming that the domestic never works on a Sunday).

3.4.5.1 Assuming the domestic does not work on a public holiday

Should one of the above prescribed public holidays fall on a day which is a normal working day for a domestic worker and the domestic does not work, she should nonetheless be paid for that day.

Should one of the above prescribed public holidays fall on a day which is *not* a normal working day for a domestic worker and the domestic does not work, she should nonetheless be paid for that day.

3.4.5.2 Assuming the domestic does work on a public holiday

The following rules apply:

- Should one of the above prescribed public holidays fall on a day which is a normal working day for a domestic worker and the domestic does work, the employer shall pay to the domestic an amount not less than (usually equal to) either:
  — a normal day's pay
  — her normal wage rate for the number of hours worked on that day, or a day's normal pay, whichever is the greater; or a third of her wage rate for the actual number of hours worked, but with a day off on full pay within seven days of the public holiday worked.
- If a domestic works on a public holiday which falls on a day which otherwise is not an ordinary working day for her, the employer shall pay to her in respect of that public holiday an amount which shall not be less than the wage payable to her in respect of a normal day's work, plus:
  — either an amount calculated at a rate of not less than her hourly wage rate times the actual number of hours worked on

that day or an amount equal to a normal working day's pay, whichever amount is greater; or

— an amount calculated at a rate of not less than a third of her normal wage in respect of the actual time (hours) worked on the public holiday, and grant her, within seven days of such public holiday, one day's paid leave (at the normal rate).

3.5 Safe working conditions

The employer is under an obligation to provide her domestic with safe and healthy working conditions. The precise scope of this obligation is ill defined, but probably extends to providing proper machinery and equipment as well as the necessary training. Accordingly, in order to comply with this obligation, the employer will be expected to ensure that:

- □ all electrical appliances and equipment are safe and in proper working condition and the domestic has received instruction on how to use the appliances properly
- □ all gardening equipment is in proper working condition, is fitted with the necessary safety components and the gardener has been instructed on how to use the equipment properly.

If the employer fails to meet this obligation, the domestic will not be considered to be in breach of contract if she refuses to work until the dangerous situation is corrected.

3.6 Annual leave

Common law. Under the common law the employer is not obliged to grant an employee vocational leave, unless expressly or tacitly agreed otherwise. The employee's common law right to vocational leave, where it exists, is contingent upon the completion of the leave cycle, usually 12 months. Thus, if the contract is terminated before the expiry of the leave cycle, the employee will, in the absence of an agreement to that effect, not be entitled to pro rata leave pay for the period worked. Further, under common law the employee has no right to leave payment in lieu of leave, so these issues are governed by the parties' agreement. The right to leave may also be conferred in general conditions of service. If an employee declines to take leave due to her she is not entitled to pay in lieu of the leave on resignation. If however the employee has not taken leave on the request of the employer, to suit the employer's convenience, the employee is entitled to be paid for accumulated leave.

Labour law. As prescribed by the BCEA, a full-time domestic worker must be given at least 14 consecutive work days of leave for each 12 months of service. Should a paid public holiday fall within the leave period, the domestic's leave must be extended accordingly, on full pay. Casual domestics do not qualify for annual leave, but regular day workers/part-time domestics do. She accumulates one day's leave for every 26 days worked.

As regards annual leave, the following general principles should be noted:

- A domestic worker is only entitled to take leave on the completion of a leave cycle (12 months). Accordingly, if the domestic has not yet completed a leave cycle (either for the first time or since last taking all leave due) and in the absence of an agreement to the contrary, she does not have the right to take leave until the completion of the leave cycle. The employer must however grant the domestic any leave due within four months of the completion of the leave cycle concerned.
- Should a domestic leave or be dismissed prior to the completion of a leave cycle, she is entitled to pro rata compensation for any leave which may have been accumulated within the last leave cycle, but not yet taken.

Your domestic must be fully paid before proceeding on leave. This includes payment for all work done as well as payment for the period during which she will be on leave.

If your domestic took days off (occasional leave) during the year, assuming that she still received her normal monthly salary, the amount of leave and accordingly leave pay which she receives must be reduced by the number of days of occasional leave which she had.

It is important to note that, except in the case of termination of employment, leave pay does not include payment in kind.

Should your domestic fall ill during her leave period (and can substantiate her claim), then she should be given sick leave for the period she was ill and be credited with the annual leave which would otherwise have been lost.

3.7 Sick leave

Common law. An employee is under the common law, not entitled to payment for periods of absence due to illness or incapacity, unless this has been agreed to. An employer may not, however, dismiss an employee for unauthorised absence as a result of illness, save where the absence continues for an unreasonably long period of time.

Labour law. As regards domestic workers, the Basic Conditions of Employment Act provides for the accrual of sick leave on full pay, in the event of absence from the workplace due to reasons of health or incapacity. The BCEA, however, does not alter the common-law position with regard to the termination of the contract where the incapacity continues for an unreasonably long period of time.

The actual number of days' sick leave which a domestic can accrue is determined by the number of ordinary working days in the domestic's work week. The number of days' sick leave to accrue to the domestic will in addition be influenced by whether the domestic is in her first year of employment or not.

3.7.1 Domestics in the first year of employment

3.7.1.1 Domestics working a five-day week or less

During her first year of employment, a full-time domestic worker working a five-day week or less is entitled to one day's paid sick leave for each completed period of five weeks in employment. Accordingly, a new domestic with six months' (25 weeks') service (working a five-day week) would have five days of sick leave on hand. If she were to go off sick for more than five days, only the first five days would be paid.

3.7.1.2 Domestics working a six-day week

During her first year of employment a full-time domestic worker working a six-day week is entitled to one day's paid sick leave for each completed month in employment. A new domestic with six months' service (working a six-day week) would have six days of sick leave on hand. If she were to go off sick for more than six days, only the first six days would be paid.

3.7.2 Domestics who have worked for more than one year

The sick leave entitlement of a domestic who has been employed for 12 consecutive months or more is worked out on leave cycles. The BCEA makes provision for leave to accrue for a maximum of one leave cycle, which is defined as being a period of 36 months or three years' consecutive service.

3.7.2.1 Domestics working a five-day week or less
A domestic working a five-day week or less is entitled to 30 days' paid sick leave for each period of 36 consecutive months in employment.

3.7.2.2 Domestics working a six-day week
A domestic working a six-day week is entitled to 36 days' paid sick leave for each period of 36 consecutive months in employment.

ACCRUAL OF SICK LEAVE		
Sick leave	**During the sick leave cycle of 36 months**	**During the first 12 months of employment**
Domestics working a five-day week or less	30 working days	One working day in respect of each completed period of five weeks' employment
All other domestics	36 working days	One working day in respect of each completed month in employment

3.7.3 Medical certificate
As a general principle, a domestic who is absent due to illness for one day is not required to produce a medical certificate to qualify for paid sick leave. As will become evident in the following discussion, there are a number of exceptions to this general rule.

An employer is not bound to pay a domestic for sick leave if she has been absent for two consecutive days or more (even if the domestic has accrued sick leave), unless the domestic produces a certificate signed by a registered medical practitioner stating the nature and duration of her incapacity. Further, if a domestic is absent from work for a single day on two or more separate occasions within an eight-week period, in order to qualify for paid sick leave she must provide a medical certificate.

If the domestic worker abuses her right to sick leave, the employer has the right to take disciplinary steps. This is discussed in chapter 6. It should be noted, however, that although the employer may consider disciplinary steps when sick leave is abused, the employer may also grant extra sick leave if she so desires.

Casual workers do not qualify for sick leave, but part-time workers do.

3.8 Medical services

There is no legal duty on employers to provide medical services for their domestic workers.

3.9 Certificate of service

Common law. Under the common law, there is no obligation on an employer to provide an employee with a character reference on termination of service. However, if the employer does give a testimonial which she knows to be untrue, she may either expose herself to a claim for damages by a subsequent employer who relies on the reference, or to an action of defamation by the employee. This is not however the position as regards employees falling under the ambit of the Basic Conditions of Employment Act.

Labour Law. Upon the termination of the contract of employment of a domestic worker, the BCEA requires an employer to furnish such a domestic with a certificate of service. Excluded from this requirement are employers of domestics who have deserted their place of employment. The certificate of service must state:

- the full names of the employer
- the name of the domestic
- the dates of engagement and termination
- the post that the domestic held
- the pay rate of the domestic at the time of termination.

Any further information the employer may wish to include, for example regarding the domestic's character, skills, experience or performance, is entirely at the discretion of the employer.

3.10 Public holidays

The BCEA prescribes the following paid public holidays as being applicable to domestic workers:

New Year's Day
Good Friday

CERTIFICATE OF SERVICE

NAME OF DOMESTIC WORKER

....

ID NUMBER:

....

Employed from: .... (date) to: .... (date)

Type of job and main duties:
....
....
....
....

WAGE at date of termination

CASH WAGE	R............
Transport allowance	R............

VALUE OF PAYMENT IN KIND:

Food	R............
Accommodation	R............
Use of land	R............
Uniforms	R............
Other	R............

TOTAL VALUE OF WAGE: **R............**

REFERENCE:
....
....
....

REASON FOR TERMINATION:
....
....
....

Workers' Day
Ascension Day
Republic Day
Day of the Vow
Christmas Day

3.11 Prohibition of certain employment

Age. An employer may not employ a person under the age of 15 years as a domestic worker.

Pregnancy. A pregnant domestic worker may not be required or permitted to work for a period of four weeks prior to the expected date of the birth of her child. She may not return to work until eight weeks after the birth of the child. The worker will be entitled to four weeks' unpaid leave before and eight weeks' unpaid leave after the birth.

3.12 Victimisation prohibited

It is an offence for an employer to dismiss a domestic worker or change her employment conditions to her disadvantage if such domestic worker:

- gives evidence on employment matters before a court of law
- gives information to an inspector
- belongs to a trade union
- takes part in the lawful activities of a union outside of her normal working hours
- discusses her employment conditions with fellow workers, her employer, or any other person
- refuses to carry out the orders of her employer if such orders are in conflict with the provisions of the BCEA.

3.13 Prohibition of certain acts relating to payment of remuneration

An employer may not take back monies paid to her domestic worker, nor may an employer give her domestic a receipt indicating that she paid the worker more than she actually did.

An employer may not fine a domestic worker or deduct an amount from her remuneration, unless by written authority of the domestic worker, or as a result of a court order or some other provision of law.

The law with regard to deductions is not limited to the two cases above: as a general principle, the employer may not deduct any money from the earnings of the domestic worker without the written authority of the domestic, or a court order, or other legal provision.

3.14 Records

The BCEA requires that employers of domestic workers keep records of:

- □ the time worked by each domestic
- □ the remuneration paid to each domestic.

As regards the keeping of these records, the employer has two options as to the manner in which she wishes to do so:

- □ maintaining records of the hours worked and the remuneration paid (this would be done on some sort of time-sheet), or
- □ entering into a contractual agreement with her domestic worker detailing the hours of work and remuneration to be paid.

The second option relieves the employer of the tedium of keeping records. Each of the above options is discussed below.

3.14.1 Daily records

This option involves the keeping of daily records covering normal hours of work and the wages payable per day, per week or per month. To comply with the requirements of the BCEA, any time sheet can be used provided it contains the following information:

- □ date
- □ intervals off work: tea and lunch breaks
- □ starting and finishing times
- □ overtime worked
- □ the signature of the domestic worker.

The Act prescribes that the above records shall be retained for a period of at least three years, and that they shall be made available for inspection by the Department of Manpower as and when required.

On page 23 is an example of a register which would be suitable for use by domestic workers who are paid monthly.

3.14.2 Detailing records in a contract of employment

Alternatively, the employer can include the details of time and wages as part of a more comprehensive contract of employment. Accordingly, if the employer and her domestic worker have entered into a formal contract of employment that details issues such as working hours, overtime and rate of remuneration, the employer is not required to keep a daily time sheet as explained above.

3.14.3 Wage register

Irrespective of whether the employer documents the time and wages of her domestic by means of a contract or by means of an attendance register, it is wise to have the domestic sign some form of acknowledgement of receipt of wages. The figure below is an example of a form the employer could require the domestic to sign on receipt of her wage.

NAME: .... ID NUMBER: ....
YEAR: 19..... MONTH: ....

Calculation of wages	R
Ordinary wages per hour, per day or per month	R
Value of payment in kind (note 1)	R
Amount due for overtime worked (including value of payment in kind)	R
Amount due for work on Sundays and public holidays (including value of payment in kind)	R
Authorised deductions	R
TOTAL AMOUNT DUE	**R**

ACKNOWLEDGEMENT:

I, the undersigned, do hereby acknowledge receipt of the monies as calculated above:

SIGNATURE: ....

Note 1

A domestic worker's wage includes the value of payment in kind, when the employer provides food, quarters and any payment other than cash to a domestic, the value of which is determined as R100 per month or an amount agreed in writing by the employer and domestic, whichever is the larger amount.

3.15 Inspectors

Employers are required to assist inspectors from the Department of Manpower in the carrying out of their inspections. It is an offence to hinder an inspector in carrying out his duties.

ATTENDANCE REGISTER

Employee name ....

YEAR: ...... MONTH: ..... Date Day of week	ARRIVAL TIME	TEA & LUNCH BREAKS				DEPARTURE TIME	TOTAL HOURS WORKED	OVERTIME HOURS	WAGE (composed of) Normal wage R ..... Transport R ..... Payment in kind Food R ..... Room R ..... Total R ..... Total Wage R	SIGNATURE
		OFF	ON	OFF	ON					
1 Mon										
2 Tue										
3 Wed										
4 Thu										
5 Fri										
6 Sat										
7 Sun										
8 Mon										
9 Tue										
10 Wed										
11 Thu										
12 Fri										

An inspector shall be furnished with a certificate signed by or on behalf of the Minister of Manpower, stating that he or she has been designated as an inspector. Only on the production of such a certificate should the employer treat such a person as an inspector.

An inspector may:
- □ at all reasonable times enter any premises which are occupied or used, or which he suspects to be occupied, by an employer of a domestic worker
- □ question any person who is or was on such premises
- □ inspect and/or seize any documents relating to the employment of a domestic worker, such as payroll records and time-keeping records.

Inspections normally occur only when there has been a specific complaint lodged with the Department of Manpower. Routine inspections are highly unlikely because the Department of Manpower does not have the resources to carry them out.

When a valid complaint has been lodged, i.e. when it is obvious that the employer is at fault or has made a mistake, usually all that is required is that the error be put right, even though the Department of Manpower has the authority to impose a fine on the guilty party.

4. *Duties of the domestic worker*

Like the duties and obligations of an employer, the duties and obligations of a domestic worker are found in the common law and the BCEA. They are:

- ☐ to enter and remain in service
- ☐ to maintain reasonable efficiency
- ☐ to further her employer's interests
- ☐ to display reasonable respectfulness and obedience
- ☐ to refrain from misconduct.

4.1 To enter and remain In service

Since the principal obligation of an employee under contract of employment is to place personal services at the disposal of the employer, it follows that the tendering of services by a domestic is a prerequisite to her right to claim payment of wages. Under the common law, a domestic worker who does not tender services, for whatever reason, is not entitled to receive wages. Conversely, a domestic worker who does tender service but is prevented by the employer from working is entitled to wages.

Once the domestic worker has entered into a contract she is under a continuing obligation to remain in service and render services as agreed until the contract is terminated.

In determining whether a certain absence or series of absences constitutes ground for termination, the courts have tended to focus on the following issues:

- ☐ The nature of the domestic's work. (The more strategically important, the more justified the dismissal. The consequences of a domestic who is solely responsible for a very sick person not arriving at work are far more serious than those applicable to a domestic who merely does cleaning work.)
- ☐ Whether the domestic's absence disrupted the normal course of the employer's household.
- ☐ The length of the domestic's service with the employer concerned.

- □ The reason for the domestics's absence (wilful absence is more serious than absence caused by circumstances beyond the domestic's control).
- □ The duration and frequency of the absences.

By focusing on the above issues, it is possible to determine the actual or possible consequences of a period of absence, and decide on the reasonableness of a particular sanction to be imposed on the guilty domestic.

4.2 To maintain reasonable efficiency

Under the common law, there is an implied condition that the employee be reasonably efficient/competent at her job. In other words, the domestic worker must be able to perform, to a reasonable degree of efficiency, that which she has contracted to do. The standard of competence an employer is entitled to expect of her domestic will depend on the capacity in which the domestic is engaged. The standards expected of a newly appointed cleaner or gardener will obviously differ from those of a domestic hired to cook and sew or an experienced gardener hired to take full responsibility for a garden. The test for the standard of competence is that of a person comparable with the domestic in question, having regard to her training, experience and any special claims or representations that she may have made regarding her competence at the time of applying for employment. Accordingly, the domestic is bound by any representations that she makes regarding her abilities and competence prior to being offered employment.

4.3 To further her employer's interests

The domestic worker is under a duty to harness her energies and skills to further the interests of her employer. She must devote all her normal working hours to the employer's "business" and may not, without the employer's permission, simultaneously work for another employer during these hours.

4.4 To show reasonable respectfulness and obedience

Respectfulness is a quality that is difficult to define with precision. In the employment context it is not to be equated with deference and obedience. The most this requirement imposes on the domestic worker is a duty to behave in a manner compatible with the subordinate position in which the employee by definition stands vis-à-vis the employer. Thus, the mere failure on occasion to greet her employer will not necessarily place a domestic in breach of her obligation to show respect. As far as common law employees are concerned, acts of disrespect directed at an employer should only be regarded as justifying summary dismissal when they are either so gross (insulting and abusive), or so frequent, as to suggest that the employee has repudiated the employer's lawful authority over her. Each case will however have to be considered on its own merits, to establish whether that inference can be drawn.

The duty of obedience differs from the duty to show respect in that the former involves an express repudiation by the employee of the employer's lawful authority. Accordingly, the failure of a domestic worker to obey a reasonable instruction of her employer amounts to disobedience. Regarding the seriousness of disobedience, in order for an act of disobedience to justify dismissal, the act must be deliberate and serious (the consequences, actual or potential, must be serious).

4.5 To refrain from misconduct

Misconduct can have a bearing on the employment contract if it is committed either before or after the parties enter into the agreement and may, in appropriate circumstances, constitute grounds for dismissal. While it is impossible to enumerate all the various forms of misconduct, the more common ones include: theft, being under the influence of alcohol, poor timekeeping, fighting, persistent idleness and absenteeism. Misconduct can take place either after or prior to the contract of employment having been entered into.

For misconduct committed after the conclusion of the contract, the courts generally consider the actual or potential effects of the misconduct on the employment relationship. As a general principle, only if the courts are satisfied that the nature of the misconduct is such that it amounts to a breach of the contract of employment, will it sanction dismissal as the appropriate punishment.

With regard to misconduct committed before the conclusion of the contract, the general principle is that there is no obligation on a prospective domestic to disclose prejudicial information from her past to the future employer. Such a duty may, however, arise if the non-disclosure of such information from her past amounts to fraud. Misconduct after the contract has become operative must generally be of such a nature as to make the domestic unfit for employment in the home of an individual or to render the continuation of the employment relationship intolerable. In other words, in terms of the common law, acts which amount to a serious breach of the contract of employment, which go to the heart of the trust relationship between employer and employee, justify the termination of the employment contract.

5. The contract of employment

As has been mentioned previously, there are two sources from which the rights and obligations of the employer and her domestic worker emanate:

- the Basic Conditions of Employment Act
- the contract of employment.

As a general rule, the common law is superseded by the Basic Condition of Employment Act, unless the agreement reached between the parties under the common law (the contract) is more beneficial to the employee/domestic than the minimum standard laid down in the BCEA.

The preceeding discussion has focused primarily on the minimum standards laid down by the Basic Conditions of Employment Act. The following discussion will concern itself primarily with the contract of employment.

The entire relationship between employer and employee (domestic) is governed by the contract of employment. This contract is therefore of vital importance, as it contains the obligations of the parties to the relationship. It is important to note that for there to be a contract of employment between two parties, there need not necessarily be a formalised, written document. A contract of employment may be an implicit one, based not on documented terms and conditions, but rather on the conduct of the parties to the relationship. A contract does not have to be in writing to be valid, but may also be entered into verbally. It may even be established by conduct, i.e. tacitly. The terms and conditions of a contract will originate from one or more of the following sources:

- written agreements between domestic and employer
- verbal agreements between domestic and employer
- implied agreements between domestic and employer. In other words, where no mention is made regarding the terms and conditions of employment, the mere fact that you pay a wage or a salary to a worker indicates that there is a working relationship (contract) between you and the domestic.

- terms implied by statute (terms contained in the Basic Conditions of Employment Act)
- terms and conditions implied by the common law.

5.1 The conclusion of a contract of employment

5.2 Validity of a contract

With particular reference to the relationship between an employer and her domestic, the following requirements must be met in order for a contract to be valid:

- Both parties must have contractual capacity.
- There must be agreement between the parties as to the intention and contents of the contract.
- Performance of the contract must be possible at the time of the conclusion of the contract.
- The contract must be lawful.

For a number of obvious reasons and in order to avoid misunderstanding and misrepresentations, the terms and conditions of employment of a domestic worker should be documented in the form of a contract of employment. Such a document ensures that neither the domestic nor the employer will be able to allege agreements that do not exist, e.g. regarding overtime pay, time off or "payment in kind".

5.3 The contents of a contract of employment

Because of the importance of an employment contract, the reader is again reminded of the following:

- The terms and conditions laid down in the contract of employment may not be less beneficial to the domestic worker than those stipulated in the BCEA.
- The fact that certain terms and conditions of employment are not documented in the contract of employment does not mean that they are not regulated in some manner. As has been explained, whether expressly documented or not, there are a number of sources from which binding terms may emanate:
  - — the Basic Conditions of Employment Act
  - — the common law
  - — the conduct of the parties.

5.3.1 Starting date (and termination date where applicable)

The starting date is the date on which you and your domestic agree that she will commence working. Obviously, if the domestic has been in your employ for some time prior to your entering into a contract, a starting date would not be applicable. The terms and conditions of the contract would in this instance become binding on the parties on the date on which the contract is signed.

In the case where a domestic is employed for a fixed period of time (for example relief work), the date or act upon whose completion the contract will expire must be indicated. When, as is usually the case, a domestic is employed for an indefinite period, no termination date would appear in the contract.

5.3.2 Job description

The purpose of the job description is to provide an explanation of the content and context of the job. The job description should provide a reasonably detailed, but obviously not exhaustive, list of the duties of the domestic worker. Typical duties would include:

- keeping the house and its contents clean and tidy
- washing and ironing bed linen, towels, clothing, etc.
- preparing and cooking meals for the household and guests
- washing up after meals
- keeping the kitchen and appliances such as the stove, oven and fridge clean and tidy
- supervising the children at all times
- assisting with dressing the children and preparing them for school
- babysitting
- maintaining the garden, including watering, mowing, raking, digging the flower beds, etc.
- planting shrubs and seedlings and fertilising the garden
- keeping the swimming pool clean
- maintaining the garden implements in good working order.

5.3.3 Hours of work

The BCEA stipulates that if the employer does not wish to keep a time register, the hours of work of the domestic worker (normal hours, overtime and meal breaks) must be contained in a contract of employment.

5.3.3.1 Total work hours

As mentioned in chapter 3, the BCEA regulates the maximum number of hours that may be worked by a domestic worker. Accordingly, any agreement in the contract of employment covering hours of work may not provide for more hours than the regulated number to be worked. Were this to be the case, then this clause of the contract would be invalid, and the regulations of the BCEA would be binding on the parties. Only when the hours of work are equal to or less than those stipulated by the BCEA, would the terms of the contract take precedence over the BCEA.

5.3.3.2 Working times

The starting and finishing times for the domestic worker should be detailed in this section of the employment contract.

5.3.3.3 Overtime

The BCEA regulates the maximum amount of overtime that may be worked by a domestic worker per day and per week. Accordingly, any agreement in the contract of employment covering overtime must not provide for more hours than the number stipulated by the Act. Were this to be the case, then this clause of the contract would be invalid, and the regulations of the BCEA would be binding on the parties.

It is however a good idea to put a clause into the contract of employment stating that the employee is contractually bound to work overtime, as and when the employer requires it, assuming that the request is reasonable.

5.3.3.4 Meal and Tea Breaks

As with hours of work and overtime, the BCEA regulates meal intervals. Accordingly, any agreement in the contract of employment covering meal intervals must not be less beneficial to the employee than the conditions laid down by the Act.

5.3.4 Remuneration

Basic pay. The monetary wage to be paid to the domestic should be stipulated. Further, the day or date on which the wage is to be paid must also be stipulated.

Payment in kind. This would include all "extras" over and above monetary wages that are to be provided to the domestic, such as:

- food
- a room
- water and electricity
- transport allowance.

Loans. Because the employer is ordinarily not permitted to deduct monies from the salary of a domestic worker, a provision should be inserted in the contract of employment that should a loan be made to the domestic, in the absence of any other written agreement, the domestic authorises the employer to deduct the monies from her salary in, for example, three equal instalments.

Increases. The employer is under no legal obligation to give domestic workers wage increases. In an attempt to avoid any confusion or misunderstandings, it should be stipulated in the contract that increases are at the sole discretion of the employer.

Deductions. Because the BCEA prohibits deductions from an employee's salary unless the employee has agreed in writing that the deduction may be made, it is a good idea to insert a clause into the contract whereby the domestic worker authorises the employer to deduct any monies owing in a certain manner. For example, it could be stated in the contract of employment that any monies owing to the employer by the domestic worker will be deducted from the domestic's salary in three equal monthly instalments.

5.3.5 Leave

The BCEA regulates the minimum amount of leave that may be granted to a domestic worker (see chapter 3). Accordingly, any agreement in the contract of employment covering leave must not provide for less leave than allowed for by the Act. Were this to be the case, then this clause of the contract would be invalid, and the regulations of the BCEA would be binding on the parties. If no mention is made of leave in the contract of employment and in the absence of any other agreement, the regulations of the BCEA apply.

Regarding sick leave, although regulated by the BCEA, the employer may wish to bring to the attention of the domestic worker the requirements regarding the provision of medical certificates.

5.3.6 Conduct

It is a good idea to attach a disciplinary code to the contract of employment, and to make this disciplinary code a contractual document by including it as part of the contractual terms of employment. The purpose of a disciplinary code is to make the domestic aware of:

- the type of conduct which is unacceptable to the employer and which will lead to disciplinary action being taken

□ should the need to discipline arise, what procedures will be followed.

Chapter 10 contains an example of a disciplinary code.

5.3.7 Termination of employment

The BCEA requires the notice period which must be given for the termination of a contract to be fair (see chapter 8). Accordingly, any agreement in the contract of employment covering notice period must not provide for a shorter notice period than allowed for by the Act. Were this to be the case, then this clause of the contract would be invalid, and the regulations of the BCEA would be binding on the parties. If no mention is made of notice period in the contract of employment and in the absence of any other agreement, the regulations of the BCEA apply.

5.3.8 Formalities

Certificate of service. The BCEA stipulates that employers are obliged to provide their domestics with a certificate of service on termination of their services, unless they desert (see chapter 3). As this matter is regulated by the Act, its absence from the contract of employment does not absolve the employer from this duty. Accordingly, the employer is required to furnish her domestic with a certificate of service, irrespective of whether such a clause is contained in the contract of employment or not.

Signatures. Both the employer and the domestic should:
□ initial each page of the contract
□ sign the last page of the contract.

6. *Disciplining your domestic*

Conflict between employers and their domestic workers is inevitable, considering the nature of the differences between them. Employers need to devise a way to handle conflict when it arises and not be caught unprepared. This chapter deals with disciplining a domestic worker. First, the following should be noted:

Because domestic workers in South Africa are not covered by the Labour Relations Act, its principles of fairness in discipline and dismissal are not applicable. This means that the employer does not need any reason to dismiss her domestic. Similarly, the employer does not have to give prior warning before dismissing her domestic. This might bring one to ask why then spend time considering the disciplining of domestics if employers are completely at liberty as to how, if at all, to discipline domestics? This chapter is provided for the employer who, although being aware that she does not have to follow any disciplinary procedures at all, nonetheless wishes to treat her domestic in a fair and equitable manner.

6.1 Objectives of discipline

Discipline has a number of objectives. The more important of these include:

- the initial correction of misconduct or inadequate performance
- the establishment of disciplinary procedures that are fair
- to ensure that discipline is consistently applied while taking account of the individual's circumstances and mitigating factors
- to ensure that the punishment meted out for misconduct or inadequate performance fits the seriousness of the misconduct or inadequate performance.

One of the prime functions of discipline and a disciplinary code in any organisation is to ensure that discipline, and where necessary dismissal, are carried out in a fair and equitable manner.

6.2 The disciplinary procedure

The employer has the right to discipline a domestic when the domestic's performance or behaviour is unacceptable. Dismissal is the most serious form of punishment that can be meted out to a domestic, and accordingly should be used only as a last resort. This does not mean that a domestic worker should not be dismissed for a first offence. Normally, the nature of the offence and its circumstances would determine the appropriate punishment. If the domestic commits a minor offence such as continual late arrival at work, just as no action on the part of the employer would not be appropriate, so too would dismissal for such a relatively minor act. In such a situation, it may be more appropriate for the employer to provide the domestic with warnings on her behaviour, and if these did not lead to any change in behaviour, then dismissal may become an appropriate punishment. If however a domestic worker is found guilty of a serious offence, such as theft, then in all probability warnings would not be appropriate, and dismissal would be appropriate for a first offence. In order to ensure consistency and minimise any misunderstanding, a disciplinary procedure covering the disciplinary process (including warnings) should be drawn up (note that this is not a legal requirement). This document should provide an explanation of the warning process as well as a basic classification of offences.

6.2.1 The purpose of warnings

The issuing of warnings for unsatisfactory behaviour is done for a number of reasons:

- ☐ to bring to the attention of the domestic worker the fact that she has committed an offence, and that such behaviour is unacceptable to the employer
- ☐ to initiate and facilitate the correction of misconduct or inadequate performance
- ☐ to provide the employer with a record of warnings given to the domestic worker.

6.2.2 The classification of warnings

Warnings are generally classified into the following three categories: verbal warnings, written warnings, and final written warnings.

The classification of warnings will, to a large degree, be dependent on the severity of the offence committed. Accordingly, in

order to be able to classify warnings, offences must be classified. Offences are classified according to their relative severity and the effect they had or could have had. Thus, the factors that determine the categorisation of offences are:
- the offence itself
- the nature of the work being done and the position occupied by the domestic
- the actual or possible consequences of the offence.

Offences are usually classified into:
- minor offences
- serious offences
- very serious offences
- dismissible offences.

Although not by any means exhaustive, the following list shows the classification of certain offences:

Minor offences
- starting late, reporting late after the lunch break
- unjustified absence from the workplace
- loafing, wasting time or deliberately working slowly

Serious offences
- absenteeism
- leaving the work premises without permission
- abusing sick leave benefits
- sleeping at the place of work
- below standard work performance

Very serious offences
- deliberately ignoring the employer's (or someone appointed by her) orders about the work
- refusing to carry out legitimate orders

Offences that could justify dismissal or suspension for a first offence
- being under the influence of alcohol or drugs at the workplace
- being in possession of alcohol or drugs at the workplace
- dishonesty or fraud
- theft
- carrying dangerous weapons at the workplace

- □ deliberately damaging property of the employer
- □ unauthorised or negligent use of the employer's equipment, whether or not this leads to damage of the equipment

Once offences have been classified, the employer is in a position to decide on the procedure to deal with each category of offence. Below is a suggested manner in which to handle various offences (as classified above).

Minor offences
1st offence – verbal warning
2nd offence – first written warning
3rd offence – final written warning
4th offence – disciplinary action

Serious offences
1st offence – first written warning
2nd offence – final written warning
3rd offence – disciplinary action

Very serious offences
1st offence – final written warning
2nd offence – summary dismissal

Dismissible offences
1st offence – summary dismissal

6.2.3 The form of warnings

It is important that employers be aware of the form that each of the various warnings should take:

Verbal warnings. The fact that a verbal warning has been given, must be recorded in writing (see paragraph 10.3.1). The domestic should also sign the warning form to acknowledge that she has received the warning.

Written warnings. As with verbal warnings, written warnings must be recorded in writing (see paragraph 10.3.2). The domestic should also sign the warning form to acknowledge that she has received the warning.

Final written warnings. With the issuing of a final written warning, the same procedure is followed as with the issuing of a written warning (see paragraph 10.3.3).

6.2.4 Period of validity of warnings

It is generally accepted that the normal validity period for a final written warning is nine months, and that for verbal and written warnings six months. However, if a negotiated disciplinary procedure provides for a longer period, or if a longer period exists through years of accepted practice, then this period is acceptable.

6.2.5 Completing disciplinary forms

Completion of all disciplinary forms and general recording of evidence are very important. The following guidelines should be followed in this regard:

- ☐ Clearly state the offence/misconduct/performance deficiency.
- ☐ State the current performance level/misconduct and your expectation.
- ☐ State the nature of the warning.
- ☐ Indicate further steps/disciplinary action which may follow if the standard as stated is not met.

7. Termination of contracts of employment

Like any other contract, there are a number of ways in which a contract of employment may come to an end. Accordingly, the contract of employment of a domestic worker may be terminated in a number of ways:

- in terms of the provisions of the contract
- by consent
- by operation of law
- because of impossibility of performance
- by cancellation for breach.

The position set out here reflects the situation under common law, since the principles of labour legislation and in particular unfair labour practices are *not* relevant when one is considering the termination of the contract of a domestic. The relevant law is the common law.

7.1 Termination by notice

It is often thought that the power to dismiss an employee summarily for serious breach of contract is the most important means by which the employer can exercise control over the employment relationship. That is not so: the employer's common-law right to terminate the contract on notice is far more powerful. Provided the employer gives proper notice (as stipulated by the BCEA), she is entitled to dismiss for virtually any reason or for no reason at all. Further, because the termination will in this instance be lawful, the reason for it will be shielded from scrutiny by the courts. In other words the employer needs no reason at all to dismiss her domestic, as long as the prescribed notice period is adhered to. Notice is a unilateral and final act that does not require acceptance.

Summary termination (no notice period given), on the other hand, at least allows for the alleged reason for termination to be tested.

7.1.1 Fixed-term contracts

Contracts of employment may be entered into for fixed or indefinite periods. The duration of the former is a determined or determinable period, e.g. a month, a year, or until the completion of a particular job. Typical of such a situation is when a "temporary" domestic is employed while the full-time domestic is on leave. In such circumstances, the temporary domestic would be hired only until the return of the full-time domestic. Where no period has been agreed to, the contract will be for an indefinite period, e.g. from day to day, or month to month. The majority of employment contracts between domestics and employers are of indefinite duration.

Whereas the right to terminate on notice is a normal part of contracts of employment entered into for an indefinite period, a contract for a fixed term may normally not be terminated on notice before expiry of the term. The contract expires automatically at the expiration of its term and no notice of termination is required. Notice may, however, be given at any time before expiry to prevent a tacit renewal of the contract. Nothing prevents the parties to a fixed-term contract from terminating it by agreement before expiry of the term.

7.1.2 Indefinite-period contracts

A contract of employment may be terminated on notice if it has been entered into for an indefinite period. The BCEA provides the following regulations regarding notice.

7.1.2.1 Notice Period

Casual and part-time domestics. The notice period for casual workers and regular day workers remains one working day either way.

All other domestics. During the first four weeks of employment, either the employer or the domestic worker has the right to terminate the employment contract with one day's notice. Thereafter, the notice period for both the employer and the domestic is one week for a domestic paid weekly, or one month for a domestic paid monthly.

A longer notice period may be agreed – and recorded in writing – between the two parties, provided that the same period of time applies to both the employer and the employee.

Notice of termination must be given on or before the 1st or the 15th of the month and takes effect on the 1st or 15th of that month. This means that if you give notice on 7 May, for example, the notice period will start on 15 May and run until 14 June.

7.1.2.2 Form of the notice

Notice under the common law may be given either verbally or in writing but it must be clear, unambiguous and unconditional. As a safeguard, it is recommended that notice be given in writing.

It may well suffice for the employer to pay the domestic's remuneration for the notice period in advance and then to terminate the domestic's services with immediate effect, instead of giving notice and allowing the domestic to work during the notice period.

In a case where the employer terminates the contract of a live-in domestic without notice, with short notice, or with payment in lieu of notice, the domestic will be entitled to accommodation for the period for which notice should have applied according to the original contract. If an employer or domestic gives normal notice of termination, it follows that the domestic would be entitled to the usual accommodation and other in-kind benefits for the normal duration of the notice period.

It should be noted, however, that the regulations of the BCEA regarding notice periods do not affect the common-law distinction between fixed-term contracts and contracts for an indefinite period, with the result that an employer will be entitled to terminate fixed-term contracts on notice.

7.2 Termination by agreement

Because the employment relationship is constituted by agreement, it may also be terminated by agreement. The domestic's consent to terminate must, of course, be real.

7.3 Operation of law

A contract of employment is automatically terminated by the sequestration of an employer's estate. Under the common law the sequestration of the employer's estate constitutes a breach of contract and the employee is entitled to be compensated for any losses suffered as a result. Sections 100(1) and (2) of the Insolvency Act determine that employees have a preferential claim on salary or wages, leave pay and bonus due but unpaid at the date of sequestration, within certain specified limits. All other claims rank only as concurrent claims against the residue of the estate.

7.4 Impossibility of performance

When a contract has become totally and objectively impossible of performance after its conclusion, the general rule is that the contract is discharged automatically and that no further liability for future performance or damages arises. If, on the other hand, the impossibility is only of a partial or temporary nature, discharge is not automatic. The employee is relieved of the obligation to perform, but the employer may terminate the contract if the period of non-performance is unreasonably long or if the impossibility is otherwise of a material nature. If counter-performance by the employer is conditional on the employee performing first or performing simultaneously, the employer may withhold performance until the employee has tendered performance. Accordingly, if either party becomes permanently unable to perform her obligations under the contract, or unable to perform her obligations for a period which is unreasonable as far as the employer is concerned, the other party is entitled to terminate the contract on the grounds of such non-performance.

7.4.1 Death of the employer or domestic

The contract of employment terminates upon the domestic's death because performance of her obligations in terms of the contract becomes totally and objectively impossible. The employer's death, on the other hand, has been held not to result in an automatic termination of the contract: the employer's estate remains liable for remuneration for the unexpired period of contract.

7.4.2 Sickness or disability

A domestic's absence from work due to illness or disability does not entitle the employer to terminate the contract summarily, i.e. without notice, unless the absence lasts for an unreasonably long period. What constitutes an unreasonably long period of time would depend on the circumstances of each case, but would revolve primarily around:

- the nature of the job being done
- the consequences of the absence.

The consequences when a domestic employed to look after an elderly person is absent from work are obviously a great deal more serious than when a domestic employed to work in the garden is absent.

7.4.3 Abolition of post or redundancy

If a domestic has been appointed for an indefinite period, the employer may abolish the domestic's post and thereby also terminate her services by simply giving the required notice. No prior consultation is required. Similarly, a domestic's job may become redundant when changing circumstances obviate the need for a domestic (e.g.the children get married).

If, however, the appointment has been for a fixed term, the employer will not be entitled to terminate the domestic's employment on notice in the absence of a stipulation to the contrary, but will remain liable for payment of wages or salary for the remainder of the term.

7.4.4 Desertion

Desertion occurs when a domestic walks out on her employer without any prior notice, either temporarily or permanently, and does not have an adequate reason for her absence. The employer is entitled to treat a domestic's absence from the workplace as desertion if the domestic is absent from the workplace, without notice, for a period of three working days or more. As far as the law is concerned, a domestic worker who deserts her place of employment is considered to have summarily terminated her contract of employment, and accordingly is treated as having been dismissed. A domestic who deserts is not entitled to notice pay. All that such a domestic is entitled to is:

- ☐ outstanding wages already earned (prior to desertion)
- ☐ pro-rata notice pay.

It should however be noted that if a domestic is absent from the workplace for more than three full working days through no fault of her own (e.g. an accident or hospitalisation) then she has not deserted her place of work.

Desertion occurs when your domestic worker walks out on you without giving any prior notice. After waiting a week to see if she returns, you employ a new domestic. Soon hereafter, the first domestic returns and demands her job back. As has been explained above, as far as the law is concerned, you can consider the first one dismissed after she has been absent without leave for three working days or more. Usually, one would wait a little longer, particularly in the case of a live-in worker if her possessions are still on the property. The only circumstances under which you would be obliged to take her back would be if she was unable to contact you due to incapacity or through circumstances totally beyond her control, e.g. an accident or abduction.

8. Remedies for breach of contract

The common law shows little concern for procedural justice in the workplace. It holds that as long as the employer provides the employee with the agreed, statutory or otherwise "reasonable" notice, she is allowed to terminate the contract for good reason, for bad reason, or for no reason at all. The employer may do this without first hearing the employee in her own defence. On the substantive side, the common law does not afford the employee any interest in her employment other than the right to be paid for availability of services.

8.1 Termination

8.1.1 Termination by the employer

The law as applicable to domestics holds that, unless the parties have agreed otherwise, there is no obligation on the employer to warn the domestic before finally dismissing her; to conduct an enquiry before dismissal; to grant the domestic an opportunity to improve her conduct or performance; to consider alternatives to dismissal; or to provide reasons for dismissal.

The law even allows the employer to justify summary dismissal (no notice period is given) of the domestic *ex post facto*, i.e. with reference to facts that come to light only after the dismissal. The only requirements are that the termination should be unequivocal and clear, and also lawful.

The lawfulness of the termination of the domestic's services depends on whether or not the domestic committed a serious breach of contract, whether the reason or motive for the termination is proscribed by statute, whether correct notice was given and whether the contract is for a fixed or indefinite period.

The law allows an employer of a domestic to terminate summarily a contract of employment, whether for a fixed or indefinite period, if the domestic's breach is sufficiently serious. If the contract is for an indefinite period, the employer is also allowed, in the absence of a serious breach by the domestic, to terminate the contract by giving the domestic due notice. But where the termination is for a reason proscribed by statute it will remain unlawful despite the fact that proper notice may have been provided.

8.1.1.1 Termination with notice

As has already been indicated, the employer of a domestic is entitled to terminate a contract which had been entered into for an indefinite period by simply giving the agreed or statutory notice. This she may do for any reason or for no reason at all. Provided that due notice had been given, the reason for the termination is entirely shielded from judicial scrutiny.

8.1.1.2 Summary termination

Summary dismissal refers to the termination of the contract of employment without notice. Whether a particular instance of misconduct justifies summary termination always depends on the circumstances of the case. Relevant factors include the nature of the domestic's job; the nature and persistence of the misconduct; actual or potential prejudice to the employer; and the employee's state of mind. What must be determined is whether the domestic's conduct amounts either to a repudiation of the contract or a serious breach of a material term of the contract, whether express or implied. Thus it has been held that habitual negligence, wilful absence from work, participation in a strike, persistent or gross incompetence and dishonesty justify summary dismissal; but not, for instance, an isolated instance of absence which does not prejudice the employer, or insolence which is not of a continuing or aggravated nature.

8.1.2 Termination by the domestic

The rules governing termination of the contract of employment by the employer apply to termination at the instance of the employee as well. If the contract is for an indefinite period the domestic may terminate it by giving the required notice. The domestic may also summarily terminate the contract in the event of a serious breach of her obligations by the employer. The domestic may, however, elect to keep the contract alive and claim specific performance from the employer.

While the remedies available to employer and domestic are formally equal, it would be wrong to assume that such equality exists in practice. Most domestics are not able to simply withdraw their services and seek employment elsewhere. For most domestics the range of alternatives in the marketplace is severely limited.

8.2 Suspension

8.2.1 Suspension on full pay

According to the law, an employer is normally not obliged to provide her domestic with work, but merely to pay wages if and when they fall due. Accordingly, the employer may lawfully instruct the domestic not to continue working (e.g. while charges against the domestic are being investigated) but to hold herself at the employer's disposal until further notice. Despite the suspension, the contract otherwise remains fully operative. Accordingly, suspension on full pay is an option which is readily available to employers. More subjective and problematic, however, is suspension without pay.

8.2.2 Suspension without pay

The common-law rule regarding termination is one of dismissal or nothing. The courts will not imply a right to suspend an employee without pay. Where no provision is made for it in the contract of employment or by subsequent agreement between the parties, suspension without pay will be treated as wrongful repudiation of the contract by the employer.

8.3 Specific performance

An order of specific performance is a court order which requires compliance with the terms and conditions of the contract of employment. Accordingly, if the employer breached the contract of employment, the domestic could apply for an order of specific performance, which if granted would force compliance by the employer with the terms and conditions of the contract of employment.

8.4 Damages

Subject to one statutory limitation, the normal rules concerning recovery of damages for breach of contract are also applicable to the contract of employment. Damages are recoverable for pecuniary loss only, provided the loss results directly from the breach, and is not too remote. The plaintiff (employer or employee) is not entitled to recover such damages as she may have prevented by reasonable preventive action. Thus, if the employer unlawfully terminated the contract, the domestic will be entitled to recover the actual loss suffered by her represented by the sum due to her for the unexpired period of the contract less any sum she earned or could reasonably have earned during such latter period in similar employment.

9. *Summary of the law*

The purpose of this chapter is to present a brief explanation of the main components of the law as it affects domestic workers in South Africa.

9.1 Wages

9.1.1 Normal time

The BCEA does not stipulate a minimum wage to be paid to domestics.

The Act stipulates that records must be kept of hours worked and wages paid, unless these issues are covered in a contract between the employer and her domestic worker.

If you do plan to keep records, these must be retained for three years.

9.1.2 Overtime

A domestic worker who works overtime must be paid at not less than one and a third times her hourly wage (including the value of payment in kind) for the overtime worked by her.

9.2 Payment in kind

To minimise confusion and misrepresentations, payment in kind should be detailed in a contract of employment. It includes items for which the domestic worker does not receive a monetary reward, but which nonetheless have a monetary value, such as accommodation and food. The rand value of payment in kind must be considered when calculating the hourly pay rate of a domestic worker. As far as the value of payment in kind is concerned, the value should be the greater of either R100 per month or any amount agreed in writing by the two parties.

9.3 Payment for work on Sundays

A domestic who has worked on a Sunday for four hours or less must be paid not less than a normal day's wage. If she has worked for longer than four hours, she must:

□ be paid wages for two days or at double her wage rate (including payment in kind) for the whole time worked by her, whichever is the greater, or

- □ be paid at one and a third times her wage rate (including payment in kind) for the time worked and be granted one day's leave on full pay within seven days of such Sunday.

9.4 Public holidays and payment for work on public holidays

All domestic workers are entitled to New Year's Day, Good Friday, Workers' Day, Ascension Day, Republic Day, the Day of the Vow and Christmas Day as paid holidays when such public holidays fall on a day that would otherwise be an ordinary working day for her. If a domestic worker works on a public holiday which is a paid holiday for her, she must be paid a day's pay plus:

- □ an amount not less than her wage rate (including the value of payment in kind) for the time worked by her on that day, or a day's pay, whichever is the greater amount, or
- □ an amount not less than a third her wage rate for the time worked by her on that day, and be granted one day's leave on full pay within seven days.

9.5 Overtime

No employer shall require or permit a domestic worker to work overtime other than in terms of an agreement concluded with her by her employer and provided such overtime does not exceed three hours on any one day and 10 hours in any week. In the case of a domestic who takes care of children, the aged, sick, frail or disabled, such overtime may not exceed 14 hours in any one week. The maximum overtime may, on application by the employer, be increased by an inspector in writing.

9.6 Bonuses

The BCEA does not refer in any way to the payment of bonuses. Whatever arrangement you have with your domestic is unaffected by the legislation.

You are at liberty to offer an annual bonus, a 13th cheque, leave bonus – or nothing. If you have an agreement with your domestic concerning bonuses of any kind, you should include details of the arrangement as a sub-section in the remuneration section of her contract of employment.

In calculating the value of the package to fix the hourly rate upon which the payment of overtime, etc. is based, do not include any bonus amount in this calculation.

9.7 Prohibition of certain acts relating to payment of remuneration

No employer shall, except in accordance with a written authority given to her by the domestic worker or in accordance with an order of court or provision of any law:

- ☐ require or permit a domestic worker to:
  - — repay to her any remuneration paid to the domestic worker
  - — give a receipt for or otherwise represent that she has received more than she actually received by way of remuneration
- ☐ levy a fine against a domestic worker or deduct any amount from her remuneration.

The employer may deduct monies owed to herself by her domestic from their domestic's remuneration provided the domestic has given her written consent for such deductions to be made.

9.8 Hours of work

No employer shall require or permit:

- ☐ a domestic worker to work for more than 46 hours in any one week (excluding overtime and work extensions)
- ☐ a domestic worker living in, to work a spread-over (from time of commencement of work to time of completion of work, irrespective of breaks in between) of more than 12 hours (or 14 hours depending on the category of domestic) on any one day
- ☐ a domestic worker who does not live in, to work a spread-over of more than 12 hours on any one day
- ☐ a domestic worker who does not live in and works not more than five days per week, to work for more than nine and a quarter hours per day
- ☐ a domestic worker who does not live in and works six days per week, to work for more than eight hours on any day (if work on one of these days does not exceed five hours, the time worked on the other days may be increased to eight and a half hours)
- ☐ a domestic who is a casual employee or a regular day worker to work for more than nine and a quarter hours on any one day.

9.9 Extending hours of work

An employer may conclude a written agreement with a domestic worker signed by both parties, in terms of which the ordinary working hours of the domestic worker, for a period agreed upon but not exceeding 26 days in any continuous period of 12 months, are extended, but not by more than four hours per week – provided that the ordinary working hours of the domestic worker shall be reduced by a corresponding number of hours during a period of the same duration as that during which the extended hours were in force, and in the same period of 12 months.

9.10 Annual leave

An employer shall grant to a domestic worker (excluding a casual employee and a part-time worker) at least 14 consecutive working days' paid leave in respect of each period of 12 consecutive months of employment with her, and a part-time domestic one day's leave on full pay in respect of every 26 working days she has worked for such employer. The leave period must, for each paid public holiday which falls within that period and which would otherwise have been an ordinary working day for such domestic worker, be extended by one working day with full pay.

9.11 Sick leave

A domestic worker who is absent from work through incapacity is entitled (subject to the provision of a medical certificate in respect of any absence of two or more consecutive days if so required by the employer):

- in the case of a domestic worker who works not more than five days a week, to not less than 30 working days' sick leave on full pay during each period of 36 consecutive months of employment
- in the case of any other domestic worker, to not less than 36 working days' sick leave on full pay during each period of 36 consecutive months of employment.

A part-time worker who is absent from work through incapacity is entitled to one working day's sick leave on full pay in respect of every 26 working days with such employer.

It should be noted that in the first 12 months' of employment a domestic worker shall not be entitled to sick leave on full pay at a rate of more than:

- in the case of a domestic worker who works not more than five days per week, one working day in respect of each completed period of five weeks of employment
- in the case of every other domestic worker, one working day in respect of each completed month of employment.

9.12 Applying for exemptions

If the employer knows and understands the requirements of the law, but has a particular need or an unusual set of circumstances, she may not be in a position to comply fully with the law. The Act makes allowance for employers faced with such circumstances to apply for permission for a certain part of the legislation to be set aside in her case. If permission is given, the employer would be granted an exemption from certain provisions of the Act. Application must be made on the prescribed form to the Department of Manpower.

9.13 Prohibition of certain employment

An employer shall:

- ☐ not employ any person under the age of 15 years
- ☐ not require or permit a domestic worker to work during the period four weeks prior to the expected date of her confinement and eight weeks after that date. The worker will be entitled to four weeks' unpaid leave before and eight weeks' unpaid leave after the birth.

9.14 Certificate of service

Every employer shall furnish a domestic worker with a certificate of service upon termination of employment except where such domestic worker deserts.

9.15 Victimisation prohibited

It is an offence for an employer to dismiss or to alter the service conditions of a domestic worker to the disadvantage of the latter by reason of such domestic worker having given evidence before a court of law or having given information to an inspector or any person entitled to such information under the Act or because the domestic belongs to any trade union or takes part in any lawful activities of such a union or having discussed her conditions of employment with her fellow domestic workers, her employer or any other person, or has refused to carry out an order of her employer that is in conflict with any provision of the Act.

9.16 Records to be kept by employers

Every employer shall at all times keep a time/attendance and wage register in respect of all domestic workers in her employment except where such employer and domestic worker have concluded a written agreement incorporating all such matters.

9.17 Inspectors

Employers must provide the necessary facilities for inspection by duly appointed and identifiable inspectors of the Department of Manpower. Any employer who hinders such an inspector in the exercise of his or her duties shall be guilty of an offence.

9.18 Approaches from trade unions

Any worker has the right to associate with a trade union if she so wishes. This does not mean that the employer is obliged to recognise that trade union in any way. As things stand at present, the employer is under no obligation to deal with a trade union and in fact employers are not required to grant a trade union official access to their domestic or their premises.

9.19 Private agreements

Private agreements existing between an employer and her domestic will only be binding on the parties if:

- they do not contradict any provision of the BCEA
- they are not less advantageous to the domestic than the Act.

9.20 Termination of contracts of employment

No reason is required by either the employer or her domestic if either party wishes to terminate the contract of employment. The only requirement governing termination is related to notice.

An employer or her domestic worker who desires to terminate the contract of employment shall give, during the first four weeks of employment, not less than one working day's notice, and thereafter:

- in the case of a weekly paid domestic, one week's notice
- in the case of a domestic paid otherwise than weekly (usually monthly) one month's notice.

If any written contract of employment provides for a period of notice of equal duration for both parties which is longer than the said one working day, one week or one month, notice shall be in accordance with such contract to be given over such longer period.

The prescribed notice in the case of a monthly paid domestic shall be given on or before the first or the 15th day of a month and shall run from such first or 15th day, and in the case of a weekly paid domestic, on or before the usual pay day and shall run from the day after such payment.

An employer and her domestic worker, except an illiterate employee, shall give notice in writing.

10. *The disciplinary procedure*

Although the Act does not require a disciplinary code to form part of the employment contract, this chapter suggests a general disciplinary procedure.

10.1 Objectives

The main objective of the disciplinary code (other than where termination of employment is justified), is to initiate corrective action where an employee's work performance is unsatisfactory, or her behaviour amounts to misconduct.

This code and procedure further aim to:

- ☐ prevent conflict through consistent, even-handed treatment of all employees
- ☐ protect the interests of both the household and the employee in matters of discipline
- ☐ ensure fair and just treatment of an employee in matters that may affect her employment record
- ☐ make all employees aware of offences which may result in dismissal.

10.2 General terms

- ☐ Formal disciplinary steps in terms of this code may be instituted in respect of: conduct specifically set out in the schedule of offences; other conduct that amounts to misconduct; contraventions of the general conditions of service or instances of incompetence or poor work performance where such incompetence or poor work performance was preceded by proper training and constructive counselling.
- ☐ The maintenance of discipline at the workplace is the responsibility and prerogative of the employer.
- ☐ The disciplinary code and procedure shall form part of the contract of employment.
- ☐ In the maintenance of discipline, the employer will ensure that all conditions of employment, legislation and rules that govern

employment in the household, and any amendments thereto, are at all times available to employees.

- The disciplinary code cannot cover every offence. The employer may exercise disciplinary action against an employee for good cause, although the cause may not be set out in the disciplinary code or the schedule of offences. This code and procedure do not deal with disciplinary action and dismissals in relation to industrial action. The employer considers industrial action to be a basis for summary dismissal. Disciplining may take the form of: a verbal warning, a written warning, a final written warning, dismissal.
- All disciplinary warnings within a certain category of offences are cumulative: an employee who is already in receipt of a verbal warning for a particular offence, and commits any other offence from that category within the prescribed period of time, will be subject to the following step prescribed for the latter offence.
- A verbal warning and a written warning will remain effective for a period of six months, and a final written warning will remain effective for a period of 9 months – thereafter the written record of the warning will be removed from the employee's file.
- Where dismissal may be the appropriate disciplinary action, a disciplinary enquiry may be held.
- Pending a formal enquiry, the employer may suspend the employee concerned from her duties. Such suspension will be effected with full benefits retained by the employee.
- An employee must acknowledge in writing that a warning issued has been received. Refusal to sign a warning, for whatever reason, will not negate the warning. Should the employee refuse to sign the warning, such refusal must be recorded on the warning. The warning must then be handed to the employee in front of a witness.

10.3 Procedure

Disciplinary steps may be taken against a worker in the household for various offences. Some offences are regarded in a more serious light than others and justify stricter action against the offender. For classification of various offences and steps to be taken, see paragraph 6.2 onwards.

10.3.1 Verbal warning
The normal action after the first minor offence will be a verbal warning by the employer. The fact that a verbal warning has been given must be recorded on a warning form, and the form must be placed on the employee's personal file.

10.3.2 Written warning
If, subsequent to the issuing of a verbal warning, the employer is still not satisfied with the performance or behaviour of the employee, or if the employee commits another offence, the employer may issue a second warning if satisfied that the domestic has been proven guilty.

The employer must explain the reason for the warning, fill in the warning form, and the employee must sign it as confirmation that she has received it.

10.3.3 Final written warning
A final written warning is justified if, subsequent to issuing previous warnings, the employer is still not satisfied with the performance of the employee, or if the employee commits another offence from the same category in the schedule of offences.

The same procedure set out in paragraph 10.3.2 above shall be followed.

When issuing a final warning, the employer shall inform the employee that should she commit an offence from the same category within 9 months, dismissal will follow.

10.3.4 Dismissal
Dismissal is an extreme disciplinary measure available to the employer. Generally dismissal may be considered if:

- other forms of disciplinary action have failed
- an employee who has received a final warning commits a similar offence and no other appropriate action can be agreed upon
- the offence appears in the schedule as a dismissible offence.

In all cases of possible dismissal, an enquiry must be held as set out below.

10.4 Procedure at a disciplinary enquiry
As the purpose of a disciplinary enquiry is to obtain a complete picture from all the relevant information, and then to come to a

fair and just conclusion and recommendation, the following procedure should be followed.

The employee should be advised of the following information and rights in writing, at least 24 hours *prior to the hearing*, and as soon as possible after the offence as is reasonable for the enquiry:

- □ the allegation(s) against her – setting out details of the misconduct/poor performance, as well as date(s) and time(s) of commission
- □ the date, time and venue of the hearing, and the employee's right to examine and challenge witnesses and other evidence led by the employer
- □ the right to call witnesses and furnish other evidence relevant to the allegation(s)
- □ the right to an interpreter if the enquiry is held in a language other than the employee's mother tongue.

WARNING FORM

Name of employee/domestic: .... Date:...........

ID no:

....

Nature of warning

Verbal warning	
Written warning	

Reason for warning being issued:
....
....
....
....
....
....
....
....
....

Was a disciplinary enquiry requested:

YES	NO

The employee's notice is drawn to the fact that in terms of the disciplinary code, a verbal warning and a written warning will remain effective for a period of six months

....
SIGNATURE OF EMPLOYEE/DOMESTIC **SIGNATURE OF EMPLOYER**

FINAL WARNING

Name of employee/domestic: .... Date:...........

ID no: ....

Reason for warning being issued:

....
....
....
....
....
....
....
....
....
....

Was a disciplinary enquiry requested:

YES	NO

The employee's notice is drawn to the fact that in terms of the disciplinary code, a final written warning will remain effective for a period of nine months

This warning is to be regarded as a final warning that your services will be terminated should you be found guilty of an offence again.

....

SIGNATURE OF EMPLOYEE/DOMESTIC **SIGNATURE OF EMPLOYER**

DISCIPLINARY ENQUIRY

Name of employee/domestic: .... Date:...........

ID no: ....

Chairman: ....

Others present at hearing:

....

....

Name Signature

Reason for the holding of the enquiry:

....
....
....
....
....
....

Findings of the enquiry

....
....
....
....
....
....

....

SIGNATURE OF EMPLOYEE/DOMESTIC **SIGNATURE OF EMPLOYER**

REPORT ON A DISMISSIBLE OFFENCE

Name of employee/domestic: .... Date:...........

ID no: ....

Reason for recommendation to dismiss:

....

....

....

....

....

....

....

....

....

....

....

....

....

....

....

....

....

....

....

....

....

....

....

....

....

SIGNATURE OF EMPLOYEE/DOMESTIC **SIGNATURE OF EMPLOYER**

Appendix: Contract of employment

CONTRACT OF EMPLOYMENT ENTERED INTO BETWEEN
NAME (print)
(hereafter called the employer)

....

and

NAME (print)
(hereafter called the worker or employee)

....

Terms of employment

Full-time ..... Part-time ..... Live-in ..... Non-resident .....

Services commence on: ....

Duties of the domestic worker
Although not an exhaustive list, the following are some of the more important duties of the worker:

- ☐ cleaning the house
- ☐ making beds
- ☐ washing dishes
- ☐ washing and ironing clothes
- ☐ preparing food for cooking
- ☐ cooking
- ☐ buying groceries
- ☐ answering the telephone
- ☐ looking after/nursing children
- ☐ looking after elderly persons

- ☐ attending to plants in the house
- ☐ taking care of animals
- ☐ washing windows, inside and outside
- ☐ any other reasonable instruction within the ability of the worker, and which is expected from domestic workers in general.

Further, the worker agrees to carry out all reasonable orders given by or on behalf of the employer, even if these duties are not stated in the above job description.

Duties of the gardener

Although not an exhaustive list, the following are some of the more important duties:

- ☐ tending the garden, weeding, watering
- ☐ planting
- ☐ pruning
- ☐ painting
- ☐ washing cars
- ☐ general work on property.

Further, the gardener agrees to carry out all reasonable orders given by or on behalf of the employer, even if these duties are not stated in the above job description.

Duty timetable

Monday: ....
....

Tuesday: ....
....

Wednesday: ....
....

Thursday: ....
....

Friday: ....
....

Saturday: ....
....

Sunday: ....

....

Working hours

Working hours will be as follows:

Mondays from .... to ....

Tuesdays from .... to ....

Wednesdays from .... to ....

Thursdays from ....to ....

Fridays from .... to ....

Saturdays from .... to ....

Sundays from .... to ....

Remuneration

Cash remuneration

- ☐ The worker will receive a cash salary of R .... per month/per week, payable not later than the last day of the month/week.
- ☐ A transport allowance of R .... per week/month will be paid for transportation to and from work.
- ☐ Salary increases are at the sole discretion of the employer.
- ☐ There will be no remuneration should the worker stay away from work without good reason.

Meals

With respect to meals and rations, the employer will make provision for the following meals on days when the worker works:

☐ Breakfast Yes No
☐ Lunch Yes No
☐ Supper Yes No

The value of meals and rations is estimated at R.............. per week/month and forms part of the worker's total salary package. However, this sum will not be paid out in cash.

Housing

- □ Accommodation will be rented to the worker or become a part of the salary package so long as the worker is in the employer's service.
- □ The accommodation will be occupied only by the worker.
- □ The cash value of the accommodation is R .... per week/month. This forms part of the worker's salary package but will not be paid out in cash and will not be regarded as compensation for overtime.
- □ The rental agreement will be renewable every month after inspection by the employer.
- □ The worker undertakes to keep the accommodation neat and tidy and not to alter anything without the written permission of the employer.
- □ The worker will be responsible for any damage.
- □ No sub-letting is permitted.
- □ Within the time of notice, the worker has to vacate the premises.
- □ At the time of employment, the following damage and faults at the accommodation are recorded:

  ....

  ....
- □ Should the worker receive visitors who intend to stay overnight, prior permission must be obtained from the employer.
- □ The employer retains the right to prohibit certain visitors from the premises and to have them removed if necessary.
- □ At the time of termination of services, or dismissal of the worker in the event of misconduct, the worker indemnifies the employer against claims for damages in respect of the premises.

Clothing

.... sets of overalls will be supplied by the employer and will remain the property of the employer. The worker's appearance will always be neat and tidy.

Pension

The worker authorises the employer to deduct an amount of R............. per week/month from her salary to be paid into a pension fund. The employer agrees to contribute R............. per week/month to this pension.

Overtime

Overtime pay is set at one and a third the normal hourly rate, and remuneration for overtime will be in accordance with the requirements of the Basic Conditions of Employment Act, at the discretion of the employer.

The worker hereby agrees to work overtime as and when required by the employer, provided that at least 24 hours' notice precedes such requests, and provided that they are within the ambit of the law.

Free time

The domestic worker is entitled to the following free time per week/month:

Afternoon free: ....
Day free: ....
Weekend free: ....

Public holidays

The stipulations of the Basic Conditions of Employment will apply.

Leave

- □ Within 60 days after every 12 months of continual service, the worker will be entitled to 14 consecutive days of paid leave.
- □ Leave not taken will be paid out at the end of the next 12 months' service at the regular rate.
- □ Workers must apply for leave at least 30 days before it comes into effect. The employer may decide, should it suit both parties, that the worker's leave coincide with that of the employer.
- □ Holiday leave will not overlap with sick leave.
- □ Leave may not be taken during notice time.
- □ A regular day worker is entitled to one day's paid leave for every 26 days worked.

Sick leave

- □ The worker is entitled to .... days' paid sick leave per year. Sick leave cannot be accrued and if not taken will not be paid out. Under the following circumstances the domestic must produce a valid medical certificate:
  — if two or more consecutive days of sick leave are taken
  — if two or more days of sick leave (not necessarily consecutive) are taken within an eight week period.

If no medical certificate is provided, the employer is not required to pay the worker for any absence related to illness.

- ☐ During the first 12 months of employment, the worker is entitled to one day's sick leave for every calender month worked. Thereafter, five-day workers are entitled to 30 days' and six-day workers to 36 days' sick leave for each cycle of 36 months.
- ☐ If the worker is absent from work for a long time due to illness, the employer is entitled to terminate the contract.
- ☐ The worker guarantees that at the time of signing the agreement, as far as she is aware, she is free of any terminal or contagious illness.
- ☐ If the worker should discover any such illness after employment, she will immediately inform the employer.
- ☐ A regular day worker will be entitled to one day's sick leave for every 26 days worked.

Maternity leave

The worker will be entitled to four weeks' unpaid leave before the birth as well as eight weeks thereafter.

Other

Time off for funerals or other urgent matters will only be permitted if the employer has given her written permission for such time off.

Duration of the agreement

- ☐ This agreement is subject to a probation period of four weeks, during which 24 hours' notice of cancellation of the agreement can be given by either party. After four weeks, one month's notice in writing must be given.
- ☐ The worker may, at the discretion of the employer, be paid out in lieu of notice.

Deductions from the worker's salary

The worker hereby gives the employer express permission to deduct such monies as are owing to the employer by the worker from the salary of the worker as follows:

- ☐ if the amount owing is less than 25 per cent of the worker's salary, in one instalment at the end of the month
- ☐ if the amount owing is more than 25 per cent of the worker's salary, in four equal instalments at the end of each of four proceeding months.

Disciplinary code

The employee hereby acknowledges that she is aware of and understands the disciplinary code of the employer, and further acknowledges that the disciplinary code (chapter 10) forms part of the contract of employment entered into between the employer and the worker.

Amendments

This agreement revokes all previous agreements and understandings and can be altered only in writing. If the agreement should be altered in any way, it will be verified by a signature.

The worker and employer, along with two witnesses, will sign the agreement and any alterations on every page. If the worker is unable to write, she should make a cross in the presence of witnesses.

Any concessions or deviations from the agreement of employment will not be regarded as an amendment of the agreement of employment.

EMPLOYER: ....

WITNESS: 1. ....

2. ....

DATE: ....

WORKER: ....

INTERPRETER (if used): ....